REACHING OUT TO THE WORLD

REACHING OUT TO THE WORLD

New and Selected Prose Poems

Robert Bly

The Marie Alexander Poetry Series
Volume 12

White Pine Press / Buffalo, New York

Publication of this book was made possible, in part, by funding from the National Endowment for the Arts, which believes that a great country deserves great art.

ACKNOWLEDGMENTS
I am grateful to the editors of the following magazines who published some of these poems: *Alaska Quarterly Review, Great River Review, Lips, Michigan Quarterly Review, Mobius, Speakeasy,* and *Triquarterly.*
Other poems, sometimes under different titles, were published in the following books: "An Open Rose" originally appeared in *Gratitude to Old Teachers,* copyright 1993 by Robert Bly.
"Eleven O'Clock at Night," "Visiting Emily Dickinson's Grave with Robert Francis," "Finding a Chunk of Wood on a Walk," and "A Bouquet of Ten Roses" were originally published in *The Man in the Black Coat Turns,* copyright 1981 by Robert Bly.
"A Conversation with the Octopus Hunter," "Looking into a Tide Pool," "Sitting on Some Rocks in Shaw Cove," "A Bird's Nest Made of White Reed Fibers," "Seeing Creeley for the First Time," "A Dead Wren in My Hand," and "A Hollow Tree" first appeared in *The Morning Glory,* published by Kayak Press, copyright 1969-70 by Robert Bly. (Acknowledgments continue on page 110.)

Cover image: Petroglyphs at Red Rock Canyon National Conservation Area, Nevada. Photograph copyright ©2009 by Dennis Maloney.

First Edition

ISBN 978-1-935210-02-3

Printed and bound in the United States of America

Library of Congress Control Number:: 2009921871

Marie Alexander Poetry Series, Volume 12
Series Editor: Robert Alexander

Published by
White Pine Press
P.O. Box 236
Buffalo, NY 14201
www.whitepine.org

Reaching Out to the World

3. SIX FRIENDS

4. THE HOCKEY POEM / 61

7. Starfish, Rock Crabs, and Sea Lions

INTRODUCTION

In his essay, "The Silent World Is Our Only Homeland," Francis Ponge says:

> In these terms one will surely understand what I consider to be the true function of poetry. It is to nourish the spirit of man by giving him the cosmos to suckle. We have only to lower our standard of dominating nature, and to raise our standard of participating in it, in order to make this reconciliation take place.
>
> *(translation by Beth Archer)*

There are many sorts of prose poems. These focus on objects in the world—a rock crab, a farm granary, a hockey game—and the changes the mind goes through as it observes them.

This sort of poem is usually written away from the desk, and in the presence of the object. Basho said, "If you want to know about the bamboo, go to the bamboo; if you want to know about the pine, go to the pine." Emerson drew from

Coleridge the idea that "every object rightly seen unlocks a new faculty of the Soul."

The prose poem form encourages the writer to stay close to the senses for the length of the poem. The mood is calm, more like a quiet lake than a sea. Its strength lies in intimacy.

Of course the writer of the prose poem cannot, despite the seeming freedom of the form, ignore the traditional poem's concern with sound. The first twenty or thirty syllables of a prose poem set up certain expectations felt in the nervous system. For example, if three "oh" sounds appear in the first sentence, intelligences below rational consciousness register these "oh" sounds, even count them, and will expect the following syllables to continue embodying the sound, or to modulate it, possibly to "ow" or "oo." Our ears hear not only vowel sounds but rhythmic units, consonant repetitions, the tunes set up by pitches, and what we could call word-color and word-fragrance. One or two sentences awaken expectations for each of these separate qualities. The poet, as he or she proceeds, has then to satisfy these expectations, or outwit them. The mind is encouraged to play with something equally playful in nature. Whatever elegance the prose poem has appears in that play.

—Robert Bly

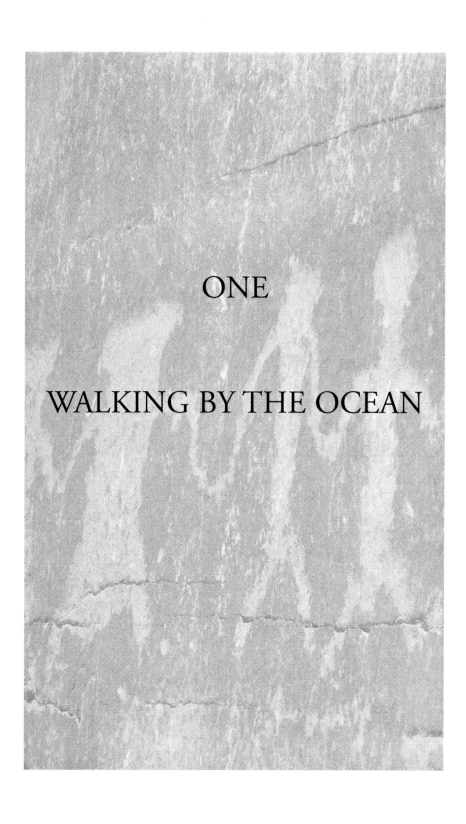

ONE

WALKING BY THE OCEAN

ELEVEN O'CLOCK AT NIGHT

I lie alone in my bed; cooking and stories are over at last, and some peace comes. And what did I do today? I wrote down some thoughts on sacrifice that other people had, but couldn't relate them to my own life. I brought my daughter to the bus—on the way to Minneapolis for a haircut—and I waited twenty minutes with her in the somnolent hotel lobby. I wanted the mail to bring some praise for my ego to eat, and was disappointed. I added up my bank balance, and found only $65, when I need over a thousand to pay the bills for this month alone. So this is how my life is passing before the grave?

The walnut of my brain glows. I feel it irradiate the skull. I am aware of the consciousness I have, and I mourn the consciousness I do not have.

Stubborn things lie and stand around me—the walls, a bookcase with its few books, the footboard of the bed, my shoes that lie against the blanket tentatively, as if they were animals sitting at table, my stomach with its curved demand. I see the bedside lamp, and the thumb of my right hand, the pen my fingers hold so trustingly. There is no way to escape from these. Many times in poems I have escaped—from myself. I sit for hours and at last see a pinhole in the top of the pumpkin, and I slip out that pinhole, gone! The genie expands and is gone; no one can get him back in the bottle again; he is hovering around a car cemetery somewhere.

Now more and more I long for what I cannot escape from. The sun shines on the side of the house across the street. Eternity is near, but it is not *here*. My shoes, my thumbs, my stomach, remain inside the room, and for that there is no solution. Consciousness comes so slowly, half our life passes, we eat and talk asleep—and for that there is no solution. Since Pythagoras died the world has gone down a certain path, and I cannot change that. Someone not in my family invented the microscope, and Western eyes grew the intense will to pierce down through its darkening tunnel. Air itself is willing without pay to lift the 707's wings; and for that there is no solution. Pistons and rings have appeared in the world; valves usher gas vapor in and out of the theater box ten times a second; and for that there is no solution. Something besides my will loves the woman I love. I love my children, though I did not know them before they came. I change every day. For the winter dark of late December there is no solution.

NOVEMBER DAY AT McCLURE'S BEACH

Alone on the jagged rock at the south end of McClure's Beach. The sky low. The sea grows more and more private, as afternoon goes on; the sky comes down closer; the unobserved water rushes out to the horizon—horses galloping in a mountain valley at night. The waves smash up the rock; I find flags of seaweed high on the worn top, forty feet up, thrown up overnight; separated water still pooled there, like the black ducks that fly desolate, forlorn, and joyful over the seething swells, who never "feel pity for themselves," and "do not lie awake weeping for their sins." In their blood cells the vultures coast with furry necks extended, watching over the desert for signs of life to end. It is not our life we need to weep for. Inside us there is some secret. We are following a narrow ledge around a mountain, we are sailing on skeletal eerie craft over the buoyant ocean.

THE DEAD SEAL

1.

Walking north toward the point, I come on a dead seal. From a few feet away, he looks like a brown log. The body is on its back, dead only a few hours. I stand and look at him. There's a quiver in the dead flesh: My God, he's still alive. And a shock goes through me, as if a wall of my room had fallen away.

His head is arched back, the small eyes closed; the whiskers sometimes rise and fall. He is dying. This is the oil. Here on its back is the oil that heats our houses so efficiently. Wind blows fine sand back toward the ocean. The flipper near me lies folded over the stomach, looking like an unfinished arm, lightly glazed with sand at the edges. The other flipper lies half underneath. And the seal's skin looks like an old overcoat, scratched here and there—by sharp mussel shells maybe.

I reach out and touch him. Suddenly he rears up, turns over. He gives three cries: Awaark! Awaark! Awaark!—like the cries from Christmas toys. He lunges toward me; I am terrified and leap back, though I know there can be no teeth in that jaw. He starts flopping toward the sea. But he falls over, on his face. He does not want to go back to the sea. He looks up at the sky, and he looks like an old lady who has lost her hair. He puts his chin back down on the sand, rearranges his flippers, and waits for me to go. I go.

2.

The next day I go back to say good-bye. He's dead now. But he's not. He's a quarter mile farther up the shore. Today he is thinner, squatting on his stomach, head out. The ribs show much more: each vertebra on the back under the coat is visible, shiny. He breathes in and out.

A wave comes in, touches his nose. He turns and looks at me—the eyes slanted; the crown of his head looks like a boy's leather jacket bending over some bicycle bars. He is taking a long time to die. The whiskers white as porcupine quills, the forehead slopes. . . . Goodbye, brother, die in the sound of the waves. Forgive us if we have killed you. Long live your race, your inner-tube race, so uncomfortable on land, so comfortable in the ocean. Be comfortable in death then, when the sand will be out of your nostrils, and you can swim in long loops through the pure death, ducking under as assassinations break above you. You don't want to be touched by me. I climb the cliff and go home the other way.

FINDING A CHUNK OF AMETHYST

Held up to the window light, the chunk of amethyst has elegant corridors that give and take light. The discipline of its many planes suggests that there is no use in trying to live forever. Its exterior is jagged, but in the inner house all is in order. Its corridors become ledges, solidified thoughts that pass each other. This bit of amethyst is a cool thing, hard as a dragon's tongue. The sleeping times of the whole human race lie hidden there; and when our fingers fold a chunk into the palm, the palm hears organ music, the low notes that make the sins of the whole congregation resonate, notes that catch the criminal five miles away with a twinge of doubt.

It has so many planes that four or five meaning enter the mind. Some exhilaration we felt as children returns. We feel the wind on the face as we go downhill, the sled's speed increasing. . . .

A CONVERSATION
WITH THE OCTOPUS HUNTER

I hear a ticking on the Pacific stones. A white shape is moving in the furry air of the seacoast. The moon narrow, the sea quiet. He comes close; a long time his stick ticks on over the rock face. Is it a postal employee saddened by the sleet? It comes nearer. I talk. The shape talks, it is a Japanese man carrying a spear and a heavy-bellied little bag. The spear has a hook on the end. What are you looking for, clams? No! Octopus!

Did you get any? I found three. He sits down. I get up and walk over. May I see them? He opens the plastic bag. I turn on the flashlight. Something wet, fantastic, womblike, horse intestine-like. May I take hold of one? His voice smiles. Why not? I reach in. Dry things stick to my hands, like burrs from burdocks, compelling, pleading, dry, poor, in debt. You boil them, then sauté them. I look and cannot find the eyes. He is a cook. He ate them in Japan.

So the octopus is gone now from the mussel-ridden shelf with the low roof, the pool where he waited under the thin moon, but the sea never came back, no one came home, the door never opened. Now he is taken away in the plastic bag, not understood, illiterate.

CALM MORNING

A sort of roll develops out of the bay, and lays itself all down this long beach. . . A hiss as the water wall two inches high comes in, steady as lions, or African grass fires. Two gulls with feet the color of a pumpkin walk together on the sand. A snipe settles down . . . then three squawks. . . . The gulls agree to chase it away. Now the wave goes out; the waters mingle so beautifully; it is the mingling after death—the silence, the sweep—so swift!—over darkening sand. The airplane sweeps low over the African field at night, lost, no tin cans burning. The old woman stomps around her house on a cane, no lamp lit yet. . . .

A ROCK INLET ON THE PACIFIC

The sea boils in over underwater rocks, then swiftly pulls back, among currents with different thoughts, everything sweeping and howling . . . Now the sea is suddenly motionless, making the holes on the rock floor clear.

But thoughts hurry in again, trying to leap up the sides; the whole inlet is like an eyeball, mad sights climbing the walls.

My own nostrils feel the bite of the salt. The sloshing water is too wild for seaweed, but limpets understand—this sloshing goes on for centuries, but no one gets tired of it . . . there is no one to get tired! The man sitting by the sea sits silent for hours, then suddenly breaks out singing. As the heart pumps, it senses the seawaters entering and leaving, jumping up and nearly touching the tern's foot. The jellyfish opens and closes, our mouth longs for the saltwater.

LOOKING INTO A TIDE POOL

It is a tide pool, shallow, water coming in, clear, tiny white shell-people on the bottom, asking nothing, not even directions! On the surface, the noduled seaweed, lying like hands, slowly drawing back and returning, hands laid on fevered bodies, moving back and forth, as the healer sings wildly, shouting to Jesus and his dead mother.

SITTING ON SOME ROCKS IN SHAW COVE

I sit in the cliff hollow, surrounded by fossils and furry shells. The sea breathes and breathes under the new moon. Suddenly it rises, hurrying into the long crevasses in the rock shelves; it rises like a woman's belly as if nine months had passed in a second. Rising like the milk to the tiny veins, it overflows like a snake going over a low wall. I have the sensation that inside me there are nomad bands, stringy-legged men with fire sticks and wide-eyed babies. These rocks with their backs turned to me have something spiritual in them. On these rocks I am not afraid of death; death is like the sound of a motor in an airplane as we fly, the sound so steady and comforting.

A bird with long wings comes flying toward me in the dusk, pumping just over the darkening waves. He has flown around the whole planet; it has taken him centuries. He returns to me the lean-legged runner laughing as he runs through the stringy grass, and gives back to me my buttons and the soft sleeves from my sweater.

THE SAND GRAINS

Thinking of a child soon to be born, I hunch down among friendly sand grains. . . . The sand grains love a worried man—perhaps they love whatever lives without force, a young girl who looks out over her life, alone, with no map, no horse, a white dress on. Perhaps the sand grains are more interested in whatever is not rushing blindly forward, the mole blinking at the door of his crumbly mole Vatican, or the salmon far out at sea that senses in its gills the Oregon waters crashing down. . . . I do sense this child soon to be born who floats inside the ocean of the womb, near the rocks, sensing the breakers roaring.

For Micah

A DAY ON THE SEA

We are at White Horse Key. It is early morning. The tide is out. Hints of "earlier and other creation" . . . and the sea, having slept all night, seemed heeded, immobile, uncenturied, robust, abundant, low-voiced. On a dead tree just off shore, a few pelicans are drying their wings and encouraging their stomach linings. As the sun comes up, they can look down and see the helpless shining fish once more.

Now a pelican lumbers shoreward. Suddenly she dives with a splash like a car wreck, then rises cradling a fish in her bill.

The day goes by. Slowly the dusk arrives. The sun settles down through the raggedy island trees. We see their heavy trunks and near us the shiny, coppery water, inflamed into further darkness by a leaping fish.

The rosy band left by the setting sun begins to go. Now the sun disk is gone, leaving behind the solitary, funereal, obscure, cloud-reflecting, cloud-worshipping, Jesuitical, altar-mad, boat-strewn Florida waters.

MANGROVE ISLANDS IN THE EARLY MORNING

We paddle in toward land on the Black Water river. It is morning! Mangrove leaves, low, red and lustrous, hover above the dark-kneed water, which slips by under the mangrove branches. The mangrove trees commingle like the language in some Elizabethan play, constantly showing their dark side and their white side, their whale side and their mackerel side.

An osprey sits on a branch sharply outlined against the sky; his white chest faces the sea. So much beauty in these mangrove islands, "hungering for life." The raggedy roots strike down, and why not? They belong, as poems do, to history, to the silence after Roland blew his horn and heard nothing back.

As we paddle along, the front trees move fast before the back trees that are moving a bit more slowly . . . ah, that is like seeing one's sins moving against the background of another's sins, those complicated stanzas in Hart Crane, where you can easily get lost and wander for days.

TWO

LIVING ON A FARM

AUGUST RAIN

After a month and a half without rain, at last, in late August, darkness comes at three in the afternoon, a cheerful thunder begins, and then the rain. I set a glass out on a table to measure the rain, and, suddenly buoyant and affectionate, go indoors to find my children. They are upstairs, playing quietly alone in their doll-filled rooms, hanging pictures, thoughtfully moving "the small things that make them happy" from one side of the room to another. I feel triumphant, without need of money, far from the grave. I walk over the grass, watching the soaked chairs, and the cooled towels, and sit down on my stoop, dragging a chair out with me. The rain deepens. It rolls off the porch roof, making a great puddle near me. The bubbles slide toward the puddle edge, become crowded, and disappear. The black earth turns blacker, it absorbs the rain needles without a sound. The sky is low, everything silent, as when parents are angry. . . . What has failed and been forgiven—the leaves from last year unable to go on, lying near the foundation, dry under the porch, retreat farther into the shadow, they give off a faint hum, as of birds' eggs, or the tail of a dog.

The older we get the more we fail, but the more we fail the more we feel a part of the dead straw of the universe, the corners of barns with cow dung twenty years old, the belts left hanging over the chairback after the bachelor has died in the ambulance on the way to the city. These objects ride us as the child who holds onto the dog's fur; these objects appear in our dreams; they are more and more near us, coming in slowly from the wainscoting; they make our trunks heavy, accumulating between trips; they lie against the ship's side, and will nudge the hole open that lets the water in at last.

WALKING WHERE THE PLOWS
HAVE BEEN TURNING

*"The most beautiful music of all is the music
of what happens"*—an old Irish saying

for Gioia Timpanelli

Some intensity of the body came to me at five in the
morning. I woke up; I saw the east pale with its excited
brood; I slipped from bed, and out the back door, onto the
sleek and resigned cottonwood leaves. The horses have got-
ten out, and are eating in the ditch . . . . I walked down the
road toward the west.

I notice a pebble on the road, then a corn ear lying in the
ditchgrass, then an earth bridge into the corn field. I cross it
to the backland where the plows turn. The tractor tires have
married it; they love it more than the rest; it's cozy with bare
dirt. We know the downturned face of the plow looked at it
each round.

In the risen sun the earth provides a corn husk in one
place, a cottonwood tree in another, for no apparent reason.
A branch has dropped onto the fence wire; there are eterni-
ties near, the body ready to see what will happen. In my
body there is a humming, it is jealous of no one. . . .

The cricket lays its wings one over the other and a faint
whispery sound rises up to its head . . . which it hears . . .
and disregards . . . listening for the next sound. . . .

FALL

Because it is the first Sunday of pheasant season, men gather in the lights of cars to divide pheasants, and the chickens, huddling near their electricity, and in some slight fear of the dark, walk for the last time about their little hut, whose floor seems now so bare.

The dusk has come, a glow in the west, as if seen through the isinglass on old coal stoves, and the cows stand around the barn door; now the farmer looks up at the paling sky reminding him of death, and in the fields the bones of the corn rustle faintly in the last wind, and the half moon stands in the south.

Now the lights from barn windows can be seen through bare trees.

TWO DAYS ON THE FARM

For two days I gathered ecstasies from my own body, I rose up and down, surrounded only by bare wood and bare air and some gray cloud, and what was inside me came so close to me, and I lived and died!

The grandfather comes back inquiringly to the farm, his son stares down at the pickup tire, the family lawyer loses his sense of incompetence for a moment.

The faint rain of March hits the bark of the half-grown trees. The honeysuckle will drip water, the moon will grow wet sailing, the granary door turns dark on the outside, the oats inside still dry.

DAWN IN THRESHING TIME

The three-bottom plow is standing in the corner of a stubble field. The flax straw lies exhausted on the ground.

The dawning sun slants over the wet pigeon grass, so that the slope of highway ditches is like a face awakening from sleep.

The oat stubble is shiny. Swaths still to be combined are wet. The farmer puts on his jacket and goes out. Every morning as he gets up after thirty he puts on besides his jacket the knowledge that he is not strong enough to die, which he first felt deep in his wooden cradle at threshing time.

GOING OUT TO CHECK THE EWES

My friend, this body is food for the thousand dragons of the air, each dragon light as a needle. This body loves us, and carries us home from our hoeing.

It is ancient, and full of the bales of sleep. In its vibrations the sun rolls along under the earth, the spouts over the ocean curl into our stomach . . . water revolves, spouts seen by skull eyes at mid-ocean, this body of herbs and gopherwood, this blessing, this lone ridge patrolled by water. . . . I get up, morning is here. The stars still out; the black winter sky looms over the unborn lambs. The barn is cold before dawn, the gates slow. . . .

This body longs for itself far out at sea, it floats in the black heavens, it is a brilliant being, locked in the prison of human dullness. . . .

THE FARM GRANARY

Sometimes farm granaries become especially beautiful when all the oats or wheat are gone, and wind has swept the rough floor clean. Standing inside, we see around us, coming in through the cracks between shrunken wall boards, bands or strips of sunlight. So in a poem about imprisonment, one sees a little light.

But how many birds have died trapped in these granaries. The bird, seeing the bands of light, flutters up the walls and falls back again and again. The way out is where the rats enter and leave; but the rat's hole is low to the floor. Writers, be careful then by showing the sunlight on the walls not to promise the anxious and panicky blackbirds a way out!

I say to the reader, beware. Readers who love poems of light may sit hunched in the corner with nothing in their gizzards for four days, light failing, the eyes glazed. . . . They may end as a mound of feathers and a skull on the open boardwood floor. . . .

SUNSET AT A LAKE

The sun is sinking. Here on the pine-haunted bank, mosquitoes fly around drowsily, and moss stands out as if it wanted to speak. Calm falls on the lake, which now seems heavier and inhospitable. Far out, rafts of ducks drift like closed eyes, and a thin line of silver caused by something invisible slowly moves toward shore in the viscous darkness under the southern bank. Only a few birds, the troubled ones, speak to the darkening roof of earth; small weeds stand abandoned, the clay is sending her gifts back to the center of the earth.

OPENING THE DOOR OF A BARN
I THOUGHT WAS EMPTY ON NEW YEAR'S EVE

I walk over the fields made white with new snow and then open the double-barn doors: Sounds of breathing! Thirty steers are wandering about, the old barn partitions gone. Creatures heavy, shaggy, slowly moving in the dying light. Bodies with no St. Teresas look straight at me. The floor is cheerful with clean straw. Snow gleams in the feeding lot outside. The bony legs of the steers look frail in the pale light from the snow like uncles visiting from the city.

Dust and cobwebs thicken the windowpanes. The dog who came with me stands up on his hind legs to look over the wooden gate. Large shoulders watch him, and he suddenly puts his legs down, frightened. After a while, he puts them up again. A steer's head swings to look at the dog; it stares for three or four minutes unable to get a clear picture from the instinct reservoir—then bolts.

But the steers' enemies are asleep; the whole barn is asleep. The steers do not demand eternal life; they ask only to eat the crushed corn and the hay tasty with dust, and sometimes to feel an affection run down along the heavy nerves. Each steer has a lamp lit inside, fluttering on a windy night.

COMING IN FOR SUPPER

It is lovely to follow paths in the snow made by human feet. The paths wind gaily around the ends of drifts, they rise and fall. How amazed I am, after working hard in the afternoon, that when I sit down at the table, with my elbows touching the elbows of my children, so much love flows out and around in circles. . . . The children have been working on a play.

Each child flares up as a small fire in the woods. . . . Biddy chortles over her new hair, curled for the first time last night, over her new joke song.

> *Yankee Doodle went to town,*
> *riding on a turtle,*
> *turned the corner just in time*
> *to see a lady's girdle. . . .*

Mary knows the inscription she wants on her coffin if she dies young, and says it:

> *Where the bee sucks there suck I*
> *In a cowslip's bell I lie. . . .*

She is obstinate and light at the same time, a heron who flies pulling long legs behind, or balances unsteadily on a stump, aware of all the small birds at the edge of the forest, where it is shadowy . . . longing to capture the horse with only one hair from its mane. . . .

Biddy can pick herself up and run over the muddy river bottom without sinking in; she already knows all about

39

holding, and kisses each grownup carefully before going to bed; at the table she faces you laughing, bending over slightly toward you, like a tree bent in wind, protective of this old shed she is leaning over. . . .

And all the books around on the walls are feathers in a great feather bed, they weigh hardly anything! Only the encyclopedias, left lying on the floor near the chair, contain the heaviness of the three-million-year-old-life of the oyster-shell breakers, those long dusks—they were a thousand years long then—that fell over the valley from the cave mouth (where we sit). . . . The inventions found, then lost again . . . the last man killed by flu who knew how to weave a pot of river clay the way the wasps do. . . . Now he is dead and only the wasps know in the long river-mud grief. The marmoset curls its toes once more around the slippery branch, remembering the furry chest of its mother, long since sunk into a hole that appeared in the afternoon. . . .

Dinner is finished, and the children pass out invitations composed with felt pens.

You are invited to "The Thwarting of Captain Alphonse"

PRINCESS GARDINER:	MARY BLY
CAPTAIN ALPHONSE:	WESLEY RAY
AUNT AUGUST:	BIDDY BLY
RAILWAY TRACK:	NOAH BLY
TRAIN:	SAM RAY

Costumes and Sets by Mary Bly and Wesley Ray
Free-Will Offering Accepted

IT TAKES SO LONG TO FINISH A POEM

My hand remembers stroking a sleek bird years ago, one which was crouching under my fingers, longing for the sky roof on top of the cabin roof, the forgiveness high in the air.

As for me, I have given so many hours to the ecstasy of detail, the shadow of a closing door, the final syllable of that poem which is already gone, looking back over its shoulder.

Well, well . . . sometimes in our slow hours a child climbs down into this world.

FINDING THE FATHER

Someone knocks on the door; we do not have time to dress. He wants us to come with him through the blowing and rainy streets, to the dark house. We will go there, the body says, and there find the father whom we have never met, who wandered in a snowstorm the night we were born, who then lost his memory, and has lived since longing for his child, whom we saw only once . . . while he worked as a shoemaker, as a cattle herder in Australia, as a restaurant cook who painted at night. When you light the lamp you will see him. He sits there behind the door . . . the eyebrows so heavy, the forehead so light . . . lonely in his whole body, waiting for you.

SNOWED IN AGAIN

Snow has been falling for three days. The horses stay in the barn. At four I leave the house, sinking to my waist in snow, and push open the door of my writing shack. Snow falls in. At the desk there is a plant in blossom.

The plant faces the window where snow sweeps past at forty miles an hour. So the snow and the flowers are a little like each other. In both there is the same receiving, the longing to circle slowly upward or sink down toward roots. Perhaps the snow and the orangey blossoms are both the same flow, that starts out close to the soil, close to the floor, and needs no commandments, no civilizations, no drawing room lifted on the labor of the claw hammer, but is at home where one or two are present.

The two people sit quietly near each other. In the storm, millions of years come close behind us. Nothing is lost, nothing is rejected. The body is ready to sing all night, and be entered by whatever wishes to enter the human body singing.

THE OLD MAN WITH MISSING FINGERS

This body holds its protective wall around us, it watches us whenever we walk out. Each step we take in conversations with our friends, moving slowly or flying, the body watches us, calling us into what is possible, into what is not said, into shuck heap of ruined arrowheads or the old man with missing fingers.

We take our first step in words each day, and instantly fall into a hole in the sounds we make. Overly sane afternoons in a room during our twenties come back to us in the form of a friend who is mad; every longing another person had that we failed to see returns to us as a squinting of the eyes when we talk, and no sentimentality, only the ruthless body performing its magic, transforming each of our confrontations into energy, changing our scholarly labors over white-haired books into certainty and healing power, and our cruelties into an old man with missing fingers.

We talk one morning about the messy lives others lead, and in broad daylight the car slides off the road. Yesterday I offered advice as I were adult; in my dream I saw a policeman holding a gun to the head of a frightened girl, who was blindfolded. We talk wisely of eternity; looking down, we see an old man with missing fingers.

A BIRD'S NEST MADE OF WHITE REED FIBERS

The nest is white as the foam thrown up when the sea hits rocks. It is translucent like those cloudy transoms above Victorian doors. It is swirled like the hair of those intense nurses, gray and tangled after long nights in the Crimean wards. This wren's nest is something made and then forgotten, like our own life that we will entirely forget in the grave when we are about to be pushed up on shore like some stone, ecstatic and black.

"DEATH COULD COME!"

For Susan Mathews Allard and Her Double Bass

The musician's fingers do not hurry at all as they climb up the Jacob's Ladder of her bass. They are not accomplishing tasks laid down by others, but have agreed to luminous labors suggested—by whom? The fingers go higher. The Cantata says: "Death is not far off. . . . Death could come!" Men's and women's voices all around cry out: "It is the ancient law!"

Now we sense the odor of roots, of partridge berries, masses of leaves that give up their lives without complaining.

The musician's fingers appear from the house of the hand-back, as if the hand were a being in itself, with its own slow joys, and its own cottage where it lives, sleeping long on winter nights.

Now the beings run up the mountain path; they are goats that do a firm dance, one foot down, then the other, many fields and mountain paths with goats on them leaping. . . . And we, who listen, are crossing a mountain at dusk. We walk a long time through the moor in the dark, at last we see a hut with one lamp lit. . . .

THREE

SIX FRIENDS

HEARING GARY SNYDER READ

Snyder stands with his arms folded while he is introduced. He is short, definitely a small horse—though not a colt. He stands quietly, sure and trained, it will take a lot to make him shy. He would never leap sideways; he might jump back, but would leap ahead an instant later. His face has something of a lion, too—the jaw curiously broad, the mouth very important. A line smiles widely, several other moats appear, one after the other, reaching far back into the gaunt cheekbones. As he reads, his eyes grow narrow and a bit slanted—it is eyes looking at something far away over the veldt grasses.

He speaks softly before the student audience, confident that he has much to say, and it is exactly what they need to know. He makes a few remarks about *Riprap* to start with. On certain mountainsides in the far west where one might want to build trails, an obsidian rock sheath is found, glassy, impossible for horses' hooves to get a grip on. So smaller rocks have to be laid on it, but carefully. So he thought that words might be used in that way, one slipped under the end of another, laid down on the glassy surface of some insight that one couldn't stand on otherwise.

He reads a poem taken from a dream: he is with friends. A lion comes out behind his friends. When he hits it with a rock, it turns into a girl. "Hail to the goddess in the lion form who swims over a river."

Sometimes he tosses his head to the side, a kind of insignificant throw, as if to say, I am one of those floating, my lily pads are not connected to the bottom. After he finishes reading a poem, he smiles for a long time at the audience, partly out of love for himself, and partly for the wonderful things he has said. He smiles actually because the poems he has written are tiny fragments of the universe, and that is what is wonderful. When he starts to read once more, he looks down—he does not have his poems by heart. They are thrown off from his life like feathers in a fight, or dropped off like hairs.

As he reads on, and goes deeper into his poems, his face begins to shine. And where they go is deeper into wells of energy, male and female energy, what he calls Shiva energy! He says Shiva is still the god with the most living worshippers. He thinks that in the 1500 BC frieze the figure is Shiva, in a Yogi posture, with antlers coming from his head. He does not read as Creeley does to each person in the audience alone. Instead, as Snyder reads, an arm encloses the whole audience—it is a swirling motion, an energy that goes in a circle around the room, and returns to him. So everyone does have a relationship—not so much with him, as with a male-female core of energy in the universe. So that the circular little globes of energy inside us are made larger as he reads.

Yet he somehow remains inside his own personality-body and can't escape. His comments are at times bookish in phrasing: "Kali, in her more benevolent aspect." When he reads some line that permanently escapes from bookishness, he swings his lion head firmly from side to side, swiftly, several times, and then swings his right foot backward for a moment and lets it fall.

ANDREI VOZNESENSKY
READING IN VANCOUVER

Andrei Voznesensky has a curious look like a wood ani-
mal, one that often lives not far from marshes, near places
where the deer sink in up to their knees. Waiting to read
while the translation is being spoken, he sits with an utterly
expressionless face—he is a pool unstirred by wind . . . hair
falling over the pale forehead is a little like birch branches
swaying over the water. . . .

His shoes are elegant Italian cowboy shoes, patent leather.
Black trousers and a blue shirt, with a folded silk tie always
to protect the throat.

He strolls slowly toward the microphone, his hands put in
slit front pockets, the thumbs pointing toward each other.
As he begins to read, his knees bend, the right hand swings
back and forth like the Neanderthal man complimenting
himself after having thrown the first stone.

He looks straight forward, bending over slightly—a fan-
tastic and resonant voice booms out, like enormous
dynamos, like immense waterfalls falling, tremendous winds
in the west sweeping up, swirling winds carrying bits of
chairs, barndoors, dust from chickenhouse floors, fragments
of wooden grave markers set up by old Carnation-con-
densed-milk-drinking trappers; the whirlwind veers off the
gravel road onto stubble fields. . . .

Sometimes the deep voice starts with a jolt, brought up
from underneath by the right arm swinging forward . . .

then it drops suddenly into the most matter-of-fact tone,
emotionless, muttering. . . .

The face has much mother-quality, his poems are mother-quality on fire, tenderness in flames, his voice is rushing water on fire, he is saying, it's OK to be on fire, OK for water, it's OK even for socialist concrete—

The voice is coming from deep in his chest that is bent forward like a javelin about to be thrown. It is the voice of some deep-throated woman shouting at last, her voice rattling the dishes, men covering their ears in the basement, or turning near the kitchen door and going back to the barn. . . . How good it feels to be able to shout about the pet chicken killed by men when you were a girl . . . to shout about the doll bureau painted with roses given to that *other* girl . . . how good it feels to shout at last!

VISITING EMILY DICKINSON'S GRAVE
WITH ROBERT FRANCIS

A black iron fence closes the graves in, its ovals delicate as wine stems. They resemble those chapel windows on the main Aran island, made narrow in the fourth century so that not too much rain would drive in. . . . It is April, clear and dry. Curls of grass rise around the nearby gravestones.

The Dickinson house is not far off. She arrived here one day, at fifty-six, Robert says, carried over the lots between by six Irish laboring men, when her brother refused to trust her body to a carriage. The coffin was darkened with violets and pine boughs, as she covered the immense distance between the solid Dickinson house and this plot. . . .

The distance is immense, the distances through which Satan and his helpers rose and fell, oh vast areas, the distances between stars, between the first time love is felt in the sleeves of the dress, and the death of the person who was in that room . . . the distance between the feet and head as you lie down, the distance between the mother and father, through which we pass reluctantly.

My family addresses "an Eclipse every morning, which they call their 'Father.'" Each of us crosses that distance at night, arriving out of sleep on hands and knees, astonished we see a hump in the ground where we thought a chapel would be. And we clamber out of sleep, holding on to the hump with our hands. . . .

SEEING CREELEY FOR THE FIRST TIME

Creeley sits on a chair, pulling up his knees to laugh, like a boy, looking very insecure, unsure, like a boy at school with pants too short. He looks astoundingly like a crow—it is unbelievable—even his hair is somehow "crow hair." Shining black, falling over his head that is full of determination to pester owls if he sees any. The beak is a crow beak, and the sideways look he gives, the head shoved slightly to the side by the bad eye, finishes it. And I suppose his language is crow language—no long open vowels, like the owl, no howls like the wolf, but instead short, faintly hollow, harsh sounds, that all together make something absolutely genuine, crow speech coming up from every feather, every source of that crow body and crow life.

The crows take very good care of their children, and are the most intelligent of birds, wary of human company, though when two or three fly over the countryside together, they look almost happy.

PUNDIT JASRAJ IN CONCERT

Pundit Jasraj, about fifty, dressed in a yellow shirt-gown, sits down. After tuning the two tambouras to the tablas, he performs prayers before beginning the concert. He brings his right hand up and lays his cheek on it; then he lifts both hands upward. Then he opens each up to receive in the palm or give from the palm. It is a four or five minute prayer in front of all. Why should he be shy? He begins to sing. His voice is faint at first, his face looks pained, the eyes closed; he is singing slowly, quietly, of something lost, something that won't ever take place again. The pain is great, the prospects not good. The lips are nearly closed. Around and above his ears white hair fluffs out—most of his head is bald. He is singing to some terrible god from a place in his chest; and it is all right, he is an artist, and he is at this same moment giving food to his ancestors in exactly the way in which they can receive it, in the way they know. The tabla player, smiling, plays with his hard fingers his morning-star tones, and waits and plays again. Now Pundit Jasraj's voice takes on a faster rhythm. He suddenly reaches out with both arms, as if to pull in the notes or perhaps catch hold of some of the pain of his abandonment that is still drifting some-where outside his body. He wants all that pain and all of God's disappointment to be inside him now. There is so much ecstasy in this; he even complains of being full. He knows that any string even slightly off tune is insulting, as well as every person who does not cry enough. All at once he stops singing, reaches behind him where the two young musicians are, takes each tamboura in turn, tunes it, and hands it back. He continues singing. Now it is sweet. Now the rhythm speeds up, deepens. Now both hands reach out again; the tabla is into its triple rhythm. He puts his head close to his mother's breast as he leans his cheek against the tamboura, and he sings about the loss, and over the loss. But only by this loss, and this detachment, can we attach to God. This pain is old, they sang this way centuries ago by the Tigris. Nothing can be done about it except to cry. Now he is pulling again and crying—he pushes, pulls, receives. He is fighting to keep insanity from coming. He pushes out with both hands and pulls something back again. He will not give in. He will keep on crying.

VISITING THOMAS HART BENTON
AND HIS WIFE IN KANSAS CITY

The stone driveway is littered with chill leaves, damp in the November mist. We climbed the back porch of stone, the door opens. A man, who looks like a short tractor, comes out saying, "Come on in here!," brushing us in with his hands. There was labor on the face; this was not the happy poet typing his poems twenty minutes a day, but the cattle driver walking through snow, the wrestler wrestling with the angel, lifting him up and driving him down to earth over and over, the joy of hard work, the thresher defeated at dusk by the weight of the bundles.

We see on the wall a painting of his—a girl with a red hood. She looks at the wolf on the path; she is hesitant; she has seen no evil, having only seen her parents, and those not well; the light brown wolf is curious to talk to her; he has met her before, in another life: she cannot remember, though he can. She does not remember, and is about to lose the battle again (although we know the wolf will twist away toward the river wounded once more).

Here are two boys in a canoe: water curves like lace around the island in the river that resembles an arm sleeping on a kitchen table; and the two farm boys in the canoe head toward the unknown falls of brightness—something they never experienced at home where their lantern at night fell on the sides of the patient Guernseys standing with their heads in prison.

Thomas Hart Benton's wife comes in, strong, radiant, triumphant, as if she had survived the flesh, like some rocket that has returned from the moon and splashed down in a

Russian meadow. Tom, as she called him, sets crouched on the sofa now, muttering strong phrases: "I used to go on tour . . . I've been all over this god damned country . . .I got as far west as Lubbock in 1934 . . . you from Minnesota? Where the damn university? Minneapolis? Hell, I've been there." His eighty-two year-old head is full of Grant Wood memories and Vachel Lindsay. "I lived on the same floor as him in 1912, maybe . . . I didn't know him well . . . in those days we were a poor a lot" . . . a gurgling laugh. . . .

There's a deep indentation in his forehead, starting near his right eye and going upward . . . above the forehead it forks, then the two forks join again deepening, and the line seems to sink into the upper sensual part of the brain.

On the wall we see a painting: girls in short skirts out in the yard during the auction sale, as the mortgage storm comes on. The hungers of some traveling preacher has flowed into the girls who have known only linoleum floors and rickety kitchen tables. The traveling preacher has confused Jesus with the storms of deep sleep. . . .

In another painting, as the woman groans in labor, wolves fade back into the woods, and the dancing girls drive their sexual energy into the ground (just as men drive nails). The energy flows down into the dead, who carry it to the throats of trees and up into the big branches, under which the half-asleep mule brushes at flies. His cock hangs down like a wagon tongue, and his long ears remind you of the long river down which we all float, sleeping and waking fitfully.

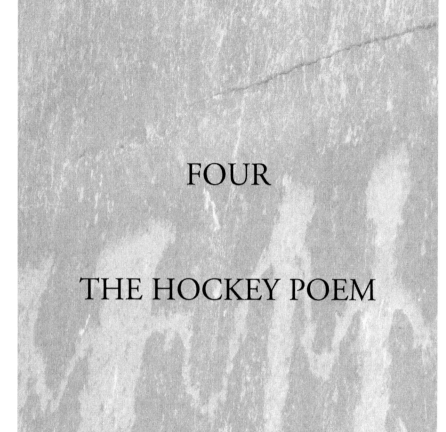

FOUR

THE HOCKEY POEM

THE HOCKEY POEM

Duluth, Minnesota

For Bill Duffy

1. The Goalie

The Boston College team has gold helmets, under which the long black hair of the Roman centurion curls out. . . . And they begin. How weird the goalies look with their African masks! The goalie is so lonely anyway, guarding a basket with nothing in it, his wide lower legs wide as ducks' . . . . No matter what gift he is given, he always rejects it. . . . He has a number like 1, a name like Mrazek, sometimes wobbling on his legs waiting for the puck, or curling up like a baby in the womb to hold it, staying a second too long on the ice.

The goalie has gone out to mid-ice, and now he sails sadly back to his own box, slowly; he looks prehistoric with his rhinoceros legs; he looks as if he's going to become extinct, and he's just taking his time. . . .

When the players are at the other end, he begins sadly sweeping the ice in front of his house; he is the old witch in the woods, waiting for the children to come home.

2. The Attack

They all come hurrying back toward us, suddenly, knees dipping like oil wells; they rush toward us wildly, fins waving, they are pike swimming toward us, their gill fins expanding like the breasts of opera singers; no, they are twelve hands practicing penmanship on the same piece of paper. . . . They flee down the court toward us like birds, swirling two and two, hawks hurrying for the mouse, hurrying down wind valleys, swirling back and forth like amoebae on the pale slide, as they sail in the absolute freedom of water and the body, untroubled by the troubled mind, only the body, with wings as if there were no grave, no gravity, only the birds sailing over the cottage far in the deep woods. . . .

Now the goalie is desperate. . . he looks wildly over his left shoulder, rushing toward the other side of his cave, like a mother hawk whose chicks are being taken by two snakes. . . . Suddenly he flops on the ice like a man trying to cover a whole double bed. He has the puck. He stands up, turns to his right, and drops it on the ice at the right moment; he saves it for one of his children, a mother hen picking up a seed and then dropping it. . . .

But the men are all too clumsy, they can't keep track of the puck . . . no, it is the *puck*, the puck is too fast, too fast for human beings, it humiliates them constantly. The players are like country boys at the fair watching the con man— The puck always turns up under the wrong walnut shell. . . .

They come down the ice again, one man guiding the puck this time . . . and Ledingham comes down beautifully, like the canoe through white water or the lover going upstream, every stroke right, like the stallion galloping up the valley surrounded by his mares and colts, how beautiful, like the body and soul crossing in a poem. . . .

3. The Fight

The player in position pauses, aims, pauses, crack his stick on the ice, and a cry as the puck goes in! The goalie stands up disgusted, and throws the puck out. . . .

The player with a broken stick hovers near the cage. When the play shifts, he skates over to his locked-in teammates, who look like a nest of bristling owls, owl babies, and they hold out a stick to him. . . .

Then the players crash together, their hockey sticks raised like lobster claws. They fight with slow motions, as if undersea . . . they are fighting over some woman back in the motel, but like lobsters they forget what they're battling for; the clack of the armor plate distracts them, and they feel a pure rage.

Or a fighter sails over to the penalty box, where ten-year-old boys wait to sit with the criminal, who is their hero. . . . They know society is wrong, the wardens are wrong, the judges hate individuality. . . .

4. The Goalie

And this man with his peaked mask, with slits, how fantastic he is, like a white insect who has given up on evolution in this life; his family hopes to evolve after death, in the grave. He is ominous as a Dark Ages knight . . . the Black Prince. His enemies defeated him in the day, but every one of them died in their beds that night. . . . At his father's funeral, he carried his own head under his arm.

He is the old woman in the shoe, whose house is never

clean, no matter what she does. Perhaps this goalie is not a man at all, but a woman, all women; in her cage everything disappears in the end; we all long for it. All these movements on the ice will end, the seats will come down, the stadium walls bare. . . . This goalie with his mask is a woman weeping over the children of men, that are cut down like grass, gulls that stand with cold feet on the ice. . . . And at the end, she is still waiting, brushing away the leaves, waiting for the new children developed by speed, by war. . . .

FIVE

POTATOES, MUSHROOMS, AND OYSTER SHELLS

A POTATO

The potato reminds one of an alert desert stone. It belongs to a race that writes novels of inspired defeat. It does not move on its own, and yet there is some motion in its shape, as if a whirlwind paused, then turned into potato flesh when a ghost spit at it. The skin mottles in spots; potato cities are scattered here and there over the planet. In some places papery flakes lift off, light as fog that lifts from early morning lakes.

The potato has many eyes, and yet little light gets through. Whoever goes inside the potato will find a weighty, meaty thing, damp and cheerful at the same time, obsessive as a bear that keeps crossing the same river. When the jaw bites into the raw flesh, both tongue and teeth pause astonished, as a bicyclist leans forward when the wind falls. The teeth say, "I could never have imagined it." The tongue says: "I thought from the cover that there would be a lot of plot. . . ."

AN ORANGE

The orange is soft and grainy. The teeth try to bite it, and then turn the orange over to the ten fingers. The thumbnail enters first, and the nine brothers hover around offering to help. The orange skin now reveals its frightened white underside, as when citizens on the border lift their faces when the tanks approach. I lift a large flake to my lips; the teeth reach for it, and the lips feel a sting for long afterwards. Maybe whoever dominates another has to put up with slightly numb lips. The fingers go on with their work, and soon the inner orange lies in the palm scared and naked.

What to do? A second later, the orange falls apart, and our fingertips feel the wet of victory. The hand holding the first half senses the mouth's instinctive greed; and modesty suggests the best solution, to swallow the naked thing. When the first half has disappeared, the hand hovers, naked itself, wet, caught in the act, not sure what to do . . . perhaps pray or reach down toward the kitchen table for the other half.

THE THUMB

My thumb is so curious bending over the top of the journal page, as I write this. It's like a calf reaching down into its manger, or a chicken looking down into a jewelry box. The soft face of the thumb is so self-assured, it can see much more than the first knuckle; it can look far down into the future of our life. Well then, thumb, tell me, where are we going now?

A MUSHROOM

This white mushroom comes up through the duffy lith on a granite cliff, in a crack that ice has widened. The most delicate light tan, it has the texture of a rubber ball left in the sun too long. To the fingers it feels a little like the tough heel of a foot.

One split has gone deep into it, dividing it into two half-spheres, and through the cut one can peek inside, where the flesh is white and gently naive.

The mushroom has a traveler's face. We know there are men and women in Old People's Homes whose souls prepare now for a trip, which will also be a marriage. There must be travelers all around supporting us whom we do not recognize. This granite cliff also travels. Do we know more about our wife's journey or our dearest friends' than the journey of this rock? Can we be sure which traveler will arrive first, or when the wedding will be? Everything is passing away except the day of this wedding.

AN ONION

The skin of the onion is shiny as a deerfly's wing, and it echoes the faint blood veins of the eyelid, the Renaissance capillaries one often sees in human skin. A wild greenish-yellow light shows through from the deeper onion. The surface shows dark splotches here and there, clouds moving overhead, darkening patches of the stubble field.

What shall we say of these lines—moving over the vast spaces of the onion—yet barely visible, like those curving drawings on the high plains of Peru. The onion lines gradually widen at its center; they catch more sunlight there, glinting with a sort of ruffian, toothy joy; after that they curve down toward the disappointed knot at the bottom. The onion lines do grow more succinct as they reach the worried fibers at the bottom. They are like the survival root of the old man, barely able to breathe, who walks with a cane, head down. He's a tough old guy, who doesn't care about you.

A DEAD WREN IN MY HAND

Forgive the hours spent listening to radios, and the words of gratitude I did not say to teachers. I love your tiny rice-like legs, resembling bars of music played in an empty church, and your feminine tail, where no worms of Empire have ever slept, and your intense yellow chest that makes tears come. Your tail feathers open like a picket fence, and your bill is brown with the sorrow of a rabbi whose daughter has married an athlete. The black spot on your head is your own mourning cap.

A CATERPILLAR

A child comes and lays him carefully in my hand—a caterpillar! A yellow strip along his back, and how hairy! Hairs wave like triumphal plumes as he walks. Just behind his head, a black something slants back, like a crime, a black memory leaning toward the past.

This worm is probably not as beautiful as she thinks: the hair falling over his mouth cannot completely hide his face—two sleeping foreheads with an eye between, and an obstinate jaw, made for eating through sleeping things without pain conscience. . . .

He rears up on my hand, perhaps looking for another world.

A HOLLOW TREE

I bend over an old hollow cottonwood stump, still standing, waist high, and look inside. Early spring. Its Siamese temple walls are all brown and ancient. The stump walls have been worked on by the intricate ones. Inside the hollow walls there is privacy and secrecy, dim light. And yet some creature has died here.

On the temple floor feathers, gray feathers, many of them with a fluted white tip. Many feathers. In the silence many feathers.

SOME CUCUMBER LEAVES

The cucumbers are thirsty, their big leaves turn away from the wind. I water them after supper; the hose lies curled near the rhubarb. The wind sound blows through the head; a smile appears on the sitter's face as he sits down under a tree. Words comfort us, the sunken islands speak to us. . . .

Is this world animal or vegetable? Others love us, the cabbages love the earth, the earth is fond of the heavens—a new age comes close through the dark, the elephant's trunk waves in the darkness.

So much is passing away, so many disciplines already gone, but the energy in the double flower does not falter; the wings fold up around the sitting man's face. And these cucumber leaves are my body, and my thighs, and my toes stretched out in the wind. . . . Well, waterer, how will you get through this night without water?

A WILLOW LEAF

This willow leaf is a long, slender thing with a dark line running down its center. Out from that center other dark lines rise over, as when in a thunder storm hay splinters begin to rise, and the crows fly off the fence posts.

The tips of my fingers remember stroking the sleek, small bird which was crouching in the hand, longing for the roof on top of the roof, the forgiveness high in the air.

As for me, I have given so much of my life to the ecstasy of detail. Well, well, well—so what? Sometimes in the wasted hours, a child climbs down into this world.

AN OYSTER SHELL

The oyster shell is whitish and rough, and resembles a chalky river bottom, scratched by rocks imprisoned in tree roots being carried down. The shell has folded in on itself in places.

If we turn it over, we see that the inside of the oyster shell is more finished, more human, more secretive. Feeling the inside with our fingers, we remember the pleasures that we have earned, the widow by the fire in her house at night, the old man in the early dawn, calling across the snow-covered fields.

FINDING A CHUNK OF WOOD ON A WALK

The rubbing of the sleeping bag on my ear made me dream a rattlesnake was biting me. I was alone, waking the first morning in the North. I got up; the sky clouded, the floor cold. I dressed and walked out toward the neighboring pasture. And how good the unevenness of the pasture feels under tennis shoes! The earth gives little rolls and humps ahead of us.

The earth never lies flat but is always thinking; it finds a new feeling, and curls over it, rising to bury a toad or a great man. It takes care of a fallen meteor or stones rising from two-hundred feet down, making a little jump for Satan and a roll near it for Calvin. As I come into the pasture, I see a piece of wood lying on the ground.

It is just a wood chunk, but it has many open places in it, caves chewed out by something. I lift it up and carry it home kitty-corner over the fields. The base is an inch or two of solid wood, only a bit eaten by acids that lie in pastures. The top four or five inches is also solid, a sort of forehead.

In between the forehead and the base there are sixteen floors carved out by the ants. The floors are light brown, the color of workmen's benches, and old eating tables in Norwegian farm houses. The open spaces in between have the heavy brown of barn stalls in November dusk.

Well, this is it—this is where the ant legions labored, the antlered soldiers awakening, their antennae brushed the sandy roof ceilings low and lanterned with the bull heat of their love. Caravans go out climbing. Soldier ants go forth over the threshold polished by thousands of pintail-like feet, their electricity for the whole day packed into their solid-state joints.

Those at home work right here, making delicate balconies where their eggs can pass their childhood in embroidered chambers. And the infant ants awaken to old father-worked halls, uncle-loved walls that still hold the sighs of the pasture, the sound of oak leaves in November, and the rustle from flocks of grasshoppers passing overhead.

Now, empty of ants, it looks like some kind of soul home. This would be a good place for souls to sit in the half-dark. If I keep it, souls of the dead in our family can come and sit there. I will keep this place for them. Some say the souls of the dead are no bigger than a grain of wheat when they come. Yet they too like to have their backs protected from the wind of nothing, from the wind of Descartes, and of all those who grew thin in maternal deprivation.

I will set out a drop of water for each of them. What the ants have worked out is a place for the dead in our families, for we too labor, and no one sees that labor. My father's labor, who sees? It is in a pasture somewhere not yet found by a walker.

THE SKULL-BONE

The bony skull is not to be fooled with; it returns a bruised knuckle to the angry fist; it wants to be left alone, and to grow impersonally and slowly, imperceptibly, to the sound of Fibonacci's flute. The skull grew in the womb as it wished; and its hunger for truth brought a fragrant sorrow to that scene in the Garden of Eden at dusk, when Adam and Eve, after having been thrown out, left weeping, hand in hand. And the skull continued to grow. After that, the woman's birth labor grew more painful, and the mother cried out sharply, while the older children withdrew into the cave corners, frightened.

Far inside the skull, embers catch fire during the erotic night, curtained by its curving walls. Say blessings on your bony skull. Its task is to keep a safe nest for the Queen of Thought, surrounded by her worker bees. Let's be grateful then for this stubborn globe that inspires the gravedigger, as he waits for the raving prince to come.

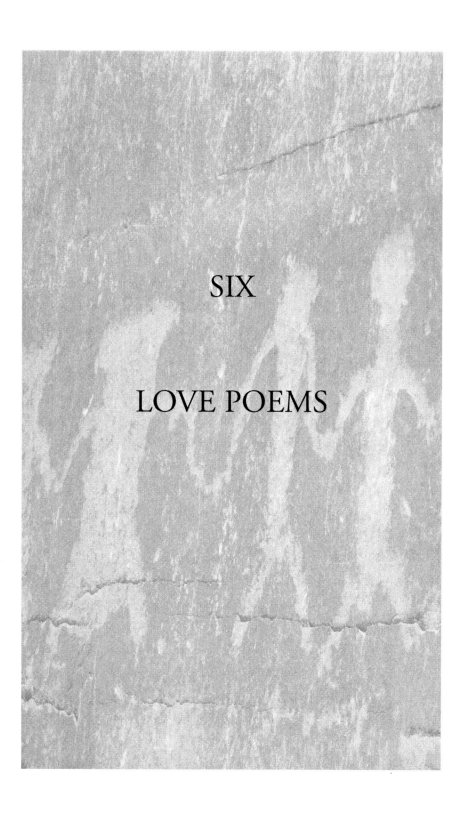

SIX

LOVE POEMS

AN OPEN ROSE

Why do we say that the rose is open? It opens as the road opens ahead of the traveler, as the water opens an instant after the diver has disappeared . . . The lion secretly feeds in the long grasses while still asleep in the cave. The grassy hollow is still hidden to which the red poppies on the slope lead us. . . . Only the pheasant's head rises over the October grasses blown by fall wind.

If I see water go over a rocky ledge, my urge is to follow after (we hear of those fatal accidents a few months after the friend dies). I feel the loneliness of "he who is not with us"— that place far inside the curling water, far inside the rose's petals. Where you go, I go. . . .

THE INNER FURNACE

We could thank the stomach first, who has learned how to magically father the children of heat. How swiftly the stomach carries into its house the loaves of carrot, onion, and brown rice, and throws these heat-seeds into the furnace, near where the furnace-keeper lies sleeping, all awash in awakening murders.

And the liver, the ilium, the duodenum, the jejunum, the caecum, the fore-gut and the hind-gut gather, secrete, comfort and hatch the new food. We are companions to the bark-eating porcupines out for their morning walk, and bosom friends with the mineral stars, whose inner furnaces heated them so well they produced their coppery light. And the thyroid and the pancreas call up the heat preserved for eras under the ice, bits of sunlight that got caught in the stone, tiny sexual flames in the sparrow's foot, the fire from the dry shavings in our tongue.

Our brains then go about warmed and fiery, so that they can take in the wildness of the cello concertos. Because of their heat, we can exchange sparks of light with another's eyes when we meet our lover on the dance floor at someone else's wedding.

A BOUQUET OF TEN ROSES

The roses lift from the green strawberry-like leaves, their edges slightly notched, for the rose is also the plum, the apple, the strawberry, and the cherry. Petals are reddish-orange, the color of a robin's breast if it were silk. I look down into the face of one rose: deep down inside there are somber shades, what Tom Thumb experienced so low under chairs, in the carpet-darkness . . . those growing swirls of gathering shadows, which eyes up near lamps do not see. It is the calm fierceness in the aborigine's eye as he holds his spear polished by his own palm. These inviting lamb-like falmers are also the moist curtains on the part of the woman she cannot see; and the cloud that opens, swarming and parting for Adonis. . . . It is an opening seen by no one, only experienced later as rain. And the rose is also the skin petals around the man's stalk, the soft umber folds that enclose so much longing; and the tip shows violet, blind, longing for company, knowing already of an intimacy the thunderstorm keeps as its secret, understood by the folds of purple curtains, whose edges drag the floor.

And in the center of the nine roses, whose doors are opening, there is one darker rose on a taller stem. It is the rose of the tumbling waters, of the strumming at night, the color of the Ethiopian tumblers who put their heads below their feet on the Egyptian waterfront, wheeling all over the shore. . . . This rose is the man sacrificed yesterday, the silent one wounded under the oak, the man whose dark foot needs to be healed. He experiences the clumsy feeling that can only weep. It is the girl who has gone down to the world below, disobeying her mother, in order to bring calm to the house, traveling alone . . . and the rose windows of Chartres, the umber moss on the stag's antlers. . . .

THE CRY GOING OUT OVER PASTURES

I love you so much with this alive and lonely body. My body is a young hawk sitting on a tree by the Mississippi, in early spring, before any green has appeared on the earth beneath. Some days walnut hollows in my chest fill with crackling light and shadows. There birds drink from water drops. . . . My body loves you with what it extracts from the prudent man, hunched over his colony of lizards; and with that it loves you madly, beyond all rules and conventions. Even the six holes in the flute move about under the dark man's fingers, and the piercing cry goes out over the overgrown pastures no one sees or visits at dusk except the deer, out of all enclosures, who has never seen any bed but his own of wild grass.

I first met you when I had been alone for nine days, and now my lonely hawk body longs to be with you, whom it remembers . . . it knew how close we are, we would always be. There is death but also this closeness, this joy when the bee rises into the air above his hive to find the sun, to become the son, and the traveler moves through exile and loss, through murkiness and failure, to touch the earth again of his own kingdom and kiss the ground. . . .

What shall I say of this? I say, praise to the first man who wrote down this joy clearly, for we cannot remain in love with what we cannot name. . . .

A DAY ALONE

This body is made of camphor and gopherwood. Where it goes, we follow, even into the Ark. As the light comes in sideways from the west over damp spring buds and winter trash, the body comes out hesitatingly, and we are shaken, we weep, how is it that we feel no one has ever loved us? This protective lamplit left hand hovering over its own shadow on the page seems more loved than we are. . . . And when I step into a room where I expect to find someone sleeping, I walk all the way over the floor and feel the bed. . . .

THE GIFT WE GAVE

This body is made of energy compacted and whirling. It is the wind that carries the henhouse down the road dancing, and an instant later lifts all four walls apart. It is the horny thumbnail of the retired railway baron, over which his children skate on Sunday, it is the forehead bone that does not rot, the woman priest's hair still fresh among Shang ritual things. . . .

We love this body as we love the day we first met the person who led us away from this world, as we love the gift we gave one morning on impulse, in a fraction of a second, that we still see every day, as we love the human face, fresh after love-making, more full of joy than a wagonload of hay.

GRASS FROM TWO YEARS

When I write poems, I need to be near grass that no one else sees, as in this spot, where I sit for an hour under the cottonwood. The long grass has fallen over until it flows. Whatever I am . . . if the great hawks come to look for me, I will be here. Knobby twigs have fallen on it. The summer's grass still green crosses some dry grass beneath, like the hair of the very old, that we stroke in the morning.

And how beautiful this ring of dry grass is, pale and tan, that curves around the half-buried branch—the grass flows over it, and is pale, gone, ascended, no longer selfish, no longer center on its mouth; it is centered now on the God "of distance and of absence." Its pale blades lie near each other, circling the dry stick. It is a stick that the rain did not care for, and has ignored, as it fell into the night on men holding horses in the courtyard; and the sunlight was glad that the branch could be ignored, and did not ask to be loved—so I have loved you—and the branch and the grass lie here deserted, a part of the wild things of the world, noticed only for a moment by a heavy, nervous man who sits near them, and feels that he has at this moment more joy than anyone alive.

THE LOVER'S BODY
AS A COMMUNITY OF PROTOZOA

This body is made of excited protozoa . . . It is with my body that I love the fields. How do I know what I feel but what the body tells me? Erasmus thinking in the snow, translators of Virgil who burn up the whole room, the man in furs reading the Arabic astrologer falls off his three-legged stool in astonishment—this is the body, so beautifully carved inside, with the curves of the inner ear, and the husk so rough, knuckle-brown.

As the body walks, it enters the magnetic fields of other bodies, and every smell it takes in the communities of protozoa see; and a being inside leaps up toward it, as a horse rears at the starting gate. When you and I come near each other, we are drawn down into the sweetest pools of slowly circling energies, slowly circling smells.

> Each living thing throws itself down before the dawn,
> And the night opens itself out behind it,
> And inside its own center it lives!

So the space between two people diminishes; it grows less and less; no one to weep; they merge at last. The sound that pours from the fingertips awakens clouds of cells far inside the other's body, and beings unknown to us start out in a pilgrimage to their Savior, to their holy place. Their holy place is a small black stone, that they remember from Protozoic times, when it was rolled away from a door.

The clouds of cells awaken, intensify, swarm; and they dance inside a ray of sunlight so thin we cannot even see it.

But to them, each ray is a vast palace with thousands of rooms. From the cells, praise sentences rise into the man and women sitting together in their room. Now do you still say there is no road?

for Lewis Thomas
and his *The Lives of the Cell*

SEVEN

STARFISH, ROCK CRABS, AND SEA LIONS

WALKING SWIFTLY

When I wake, I hear sheep eating apple peels just outside the screen. The trees are heavy, soaked, cold and hushed, the sun just rising. All seems calm, and yet somewhere inside I am not calm. We live in wooden buildings made of two-by-fours, making the landscape nervous for a hundred miles. And the Emperor when he was sixty called for rhinoceros horn, for sky-blue phoenix eggs shaped from veined rock, dipped in rooster blood. Around him the wasps kept guard, the hens continued their patrol, the oysters opened and closed all questions. The heat inside the human body grows, it does not know where to throw itself—for a while it knots into will, heavy, burning, sweet, then into generosity, that longs to take on the burdens of others, and then into mad love that lasts forever. The sculptor walks swiftly to his studio, and carves oceanic waves into the dragon's mane.

THE STARFISH

It is low tide. Fog. I have climbed down the cliffs from Pierce Ranch to the tide pools. Now the ecstasy of the low tide, kneeling down, alone. In six inches of clear water I notice a purple starfish—with nineteen arms! It is a delicate purple, the color of old carbon paper, or an attic dress . . . at the webs between the arms sometimes a more intense sunset red glows through. The fingers are relaxed . . . some curled up at the tips . . . with delicate rods . . . apparently globes on top of each, as at World's Fairs, waving about. The starfish slowly moves up the groin of the rock . . . then back down . . . many of its arms rolled up now, lazily, like a puppy on its back. One arm is especially active and curved up over its own body as if a dinosaur were looking behind him.

Slow slowly and evenly it moves! The starfish is a glacier, going sixty miles a year! It moves over the pink rock, by means I cannot see . . . and into marvelously floating delicate brown weeds. It is about the size of the bottom of a pail. When I reach into it, it tightens and then slowly relaxes. . . . I take an arm and quickly lift. The underside is a pale tan. . . . Gradually, as I watch, thousands of tiny tubes begin rising from all over the underside . . . hundreds in the mouth, hundreds along the nineteen underarms . . . all looking . . . feeling . . . like a man looking for a woman . . . tiny heads blindly feeling for a rock and finding only air. A purple rim runs along the underside of every arm, with paler tubes. Probably its moving-feet.

I put him back in. He unfolds—I had forgotten how purple he was—and slides down into his rock groin, the snaillike feelers waving as if nothing had happened, and nothing has.

A MOTH

I feel something brush my knuckle, and open my eyes. The moth's skinny legs are crooked as cottonwood twigs. Its wings are tan, like a pitchfork handle showing through the hay, but in parts a deeper brown, the color of chopped tobacco loved by old men. Circles that look like eyes decorate the wings. And some airs flow around the tubular body just as currents of air flow around the fuselage.

The wings are serrated and have battlements. The moth leans its antennae over . . . and the long searcher touches the skin. The skin feels each touch for long afterward.

As the moth touches me, I remember last night's dream. A car pulled up close behind. "Oh, oh, we have visitors," I said. The Plymouth pulled past, and it was not the police, but a speeding car that a moment later turned and crashed into the trees. The passengers in the back seat—all of them masked—sat motionless, facing toward the road already passed.

SOME SEA LIONS

for Michael and Barbara Whitt

The blue sky suddenly gone—fog. We cut the engine and drift. We glimpse a derrick on shore. No, it is a bird—a Great Blue Heron. He turns his head and walks away . . . like some old Hittite empire, all the brutality forgotten. Only the rare vases left, and the elegant necks of the women.

Sea lions float nearby. Whiskered heads peer over at us attentively like angels called to look at a baby. They have risen from their sea-mangers to peer at us. It's clear their magi come to them every day, and they gaze at the godless in their wooden boat. . . .

The boulders we see on shore turn out to be sea lions, hundreds of them! Some are sleeping, others float on their backs playing. Soon the whole shore starts to roll seaward, barking and flapping.

Now the sea lions are everywhere in the water underneath us. One sleek head pops up five feet from the boat, looking neither arrogant nor surprised, but like a billfold found in the water, or a mountain that has been rained on for three weeks.

A MARRIED MAN LOOKING AT A CHERRY TREE

Cherry boughs in blossom sway in the night wind, resembling conductors' hands that follow the note just about to come. The clumps of blossoms bend, forgive, and return petals to the earth.

And we, who are married, sway like these boughs, as if in heavy canyons, moving upstream against the tiny cedar twigs being turned over and over in the cloudy spring river coming down.

I climbed down today from the cliffs to the black mussels and back. Now I am standing in the dark, looking at the cherry branches above me sway against the night sky not far from the sea.

A PINE TREE

My friend, this body goes on and on through the piney-woods. I don't know where we are. . . . I know only that sometimes I love the trunk of a pine, and if I go that way, I admire the grandeur of created things, the stout pillars, roofed with a marble band, and I walk into the courtyard of a wooden temple, and a woman comes with me.

I hear on the instrument of my body what is remembered and forgotten a thousand times. It doesn't matter what happens to us as we grow old. We have experienced enough grandeur already, snow falling on top of other snow, the fishermen kneeling beside a wood fire, the words inside a poem coming sweetly to a close.

THE COUPLE I DO NOT KNOW
SITTING BY THE SHORE NEAR CARMEL

A woman chats with a man while they sit on a rock above the sea. I surmise that the man is talking about things perceptible to him; but the woman, as she looks out over the sea, knows that a child is approaching. The sun setting behind Point Lobos makes the water surface gleamy, glowing, rolling; the sea lifts on invisible shoulders, silvery, dangerous, tense, furred with seaweed hide, silent, luminous in its golden light-patches, glorified by all that is gone and absent; and the persistent waters push on through and above the offshore rocks, and more behind, more rising.

A woman chats with a man. They both know that the ocean will give birth to the night, whatever we do; and the sun will set behind Point Lobos.

THE SKIN ON A HORSE'S NECK

Sometimes the skin of a horse's neck longs for a hoofless hand to stroke its deep-toned muscles, as a cat longs for a hand to touch the thunderstorm hidden below its silky hide. Have we praised enough the swiftness with which the skin sends out its messages, the music that goes palm to palm, stomach to stomach, foot sole to foot sole.

The horse's skin knows the coolness of the rain in the next county, knows when a hawk is flying overhead, leaving its moving shadow on the horse's neck.

THE ROCK CRAB

A rock crab sits heavily on a mess of greenish-brown sea-weed; ocean water still gleams on his shell. He is matter, sub-stantiality, accidentia, a heavy downpouring of primitive light. The mottled shapes on his top suggest desert forts.

Whenever I lean down and inhale his odor I feel vulnerable, as when one recalls at noon a detail from last night's dream.

My hand reaches out and turns him over, and we all can see his underside, as fierce as the underside of the Sahara. The six claws folded over the stomach are joined segments of what has to be done, hard bits of necessity. His will is strong, living without mother or father, bony, unsentimental, even on his upper legs that slope like arms. Inside the shelled arms there is cold and muscular flesh, still visionary, washed at night when sea water carries its moony splashing through the claw tunnel.

THE MOON TRAVELING ALONE

The sun goes down, each minute the air darker. The night thickens, pulls the earth down to it. And if my body is earth, then what? Then I am down here thickening as night comes on. Earth has earth things, earthly, joined. They snuggle down in one den, one manger; one sweep of arms holds them, one clump of pine. Owlets sit together in one hollow tree.

But when night has truly come, the sun will drop down below the earth, and travel sizzling along the underneath-ocean-darkness path. There a hundred developed saints lie stretched out, throwing bits of darkness onto the road.

As for the moon, it will go on traveling alone over the darkened earth all night, slipping through arms reached up to it.

A SALAMANDER

Walking. Afternoon. The war still going on, I stoop down to pick up a salamander. He is halfway across the mossy forest path. He is dark brown, fantastically cold in my hand. This one is new to me—the upper part of his eyeball light green . . . strange bullfrog eyes. The belly is brilliant orange, color of airplane gasoline on fire; the back is a heavy-duty rubber black, with goose pimples from permanent cold. I make a kind of pulpit of my left hand, and turn him gently upright; his head and front legs look out at me, as his hands rest on my crossing thumb joint. Warmed, he grows lively, pulls himself out, and falls to earth, where he raises his chin defiantly. I pick him up again. But he is patient, this war. I hold him again between thumb and forefinger for many minutes, and his front paws hold on to my thumb resignedly— perhaps I could hold him so for hours. Perhaps he could be held gently this way for days until he died, the green eyes still opening and closing. When I turn my wrist over, I see the long orange-black tail hanging down into the cathedral of the open palm, circling back and forth, rolling and unrolling like a snake. It hangs down like a rudder on some immensely long boat, a rudder that the men and women on board looking over the handrail do not see.

ELEPHANTS IN KENYA

Just in front of us we glimpse three elephants—twenty yards or so away. The white tusks show first, gleaming just above the long grass, then a glimpse of some immense thing, then the great ears flapping.

The massive elephant lifts her trunk-end up, stuffs grass in, moves on, stuffs more in, to the sound of crackling tree branches. One front leg lifts, and then the other. This massive one doesn't know we are here; she slowly turns and walks toward us. She looks big, confident, her whole fore-quarters full of character. Now she turns sideways; she takes in a low branch, then turns again in our direction. It all goes so slowly. The bones in her hip joints roll slowly. We all grow old slowly. The night passes so slowly, but it's all right, dawn always comes. What is eternal arrives in the same way, without moving, all at once.

With her ears flapping, she seems to be some huge sea animal—as if the elephants were walking in an enormous sea garden, as if the sweet African air were all ocean, as if this patient feeding were taking place in the slowness of water.

Several younger elephants hurry in from the left, babies with them, and abruptly a massive adult arrives with huge tusks. Two more adults enter the clearing, moving eastward. Thad says a silent communication has taken place: The It is near. Time to leave. And they are gone.

CLIMBING UP MOUNT VISION
WITH MY LITTLE BOY

For Noah

We started up. All the way he held my hand. Sometimes he falls back to bend over a banana slug, then senses how lonely the slug is, and comes running back. He never complained, and we went straight up. How much I love being with him! How much I love to feel his small leafy hand curl around my finger. He holds on, and we are flying through a cloud. On top we hunker down beneath some bushes to get out of the wind, while the girls go off to play, and he tells me the story of the little boy who wouldn't cut off his hair and give it to a witch, and so she changed him into a hollow log. A boy and girl came along, and stepped on the log—and the log said, "Oww!" They put their feet on it again, and the log said, "Oww!" Then they looked inside and saw a boy's jacket sticking out. A little boy was in there! "I can't come out, I've been changed into a hollow log." That's the end, he said.

Then I remembered a bit more—the boy and the girl went to a wise man . . . he corrected me, "It was a wise woman, Daddy," . . . and said, "How can we get him changed back into a little boy?" She said, "Here is a pearl. If a crow asks you for it, give it to him." So they went along. Pretty soon a crow came and said, "Can I have the buttons on your shirt?" The boy said, "Yes." Then the crow said, "Can I have that pearl in your shirt pocket?" "Yes." Then the crow flew up and dropped some moss down the witch's chimney. The chimney got full, the witch started to cough. The crow dropped in some more moss. Then the witch had to open the door, and run outside! Then the crow took an oyster, a big one, from the Johnson Oyster Company, and flew high into the air, and dropped it right on the witch's head. And that was the end of her. And then the boy was changed back again into a little boy.

"That's the end," he said.

The Author

Robert Bly has published over twenty books of poems and translations. His most recent book is his translations of Hafez (with Leonard Lewisohn), *Angels Knocking at the Tavern Door* with HarperCollins. He has been one of the prime advocates in America of the prose poem as a literary form; his collections of prose poems have been published as *The Morning Glory, This Body Is Made of Camphor and Gopherwood,* and *What Have I Ever Lost by Dying?*

He has also been a strong advocate of translation of European and South American poets. He has done extensive translations of Pablo Neruda, Rainer Marie Rilke, Tomas Tranströmer, Rolf Jacobsen, and others. His two most recent book of poems are ghazals collected in *The Night Abraham Called to the Stars,* and *My Sentence Was a Thousand Years of Joy.*

Acknowledgments (continued from copyright page)

"A Rock Inlet on the Pacific," "August Rain," "Opening the Door of a Barn I Thought Was Empty on New Year's Eve," "Andrei Voznesensky Reading in Vancouver," "Visiting Thomas Hart Benton and His Wife in Kansas City," "The Hockey Poem," "A Caterpillar," "Grass from Two Years," and "A Married Man Looking at a Cherry Tree" were included in an enlarged edition of *The Morning Glory* published by Harper & Row in 1975.

"November Day at McClure's Beach," "The Dead Seal," "Calm Morning," "The Sand Grains," "The Starfish," "Some Sea Lions," "A Salamander," and "Climbing Up Mount Vision with My Little Boy" were first published as *Point Reyes Poems* by Mudra Press, 1974, reprinted later by Floating Island Press.

"Fall" and "Sunset at a Lake" originally appeared in *Silence in the Snowy Fields*, copyright 1962 by Robert Bly

"Two Days on the Farm," "Going Out to Check the Ewes," "Coming in for Supper," "Finding the Father," "Snowed in Again," "The Old Man with Missing Fingers," "Some Cucumber Leaves," "The Cry Going Out Over Pastures," "A Day Alone," "The Gift We Gave," "The Lover's Body as a Community of Protozoa," "Walking Swiftly" and "The Moon Traveling Alone" originally appeared in *This Body Is Made of Camphor and Gopherwood*, copyright 1977 by Robert Bly.

"Walking Where the Plows Have Been Turning" and "Dawn in Threshing Time" originally appeared in *This Tree Will Be Here for a Thousand Years*, copyright 1979 by Robert Bly.

"Finding a Chunk of Amethyst," "A Potato," "An Orange," "A Mushroom," and "The Rock Crab" first appeared in *Ten Poems of Francis Ponge Translated by Robert Bly* and *Ten Poems of Robert Bly Inspired by the Poems of Francis Ponge*, copyright 1990 by Robert Bly (Owl's Head Press, New Brunswick, Canada).

"The Farm Granary," "Death Could Come!," "A Moth," and "The Couple I Do Not Know Sitting by the Shore Near Carmel" originally appeared in What Have I Ever Lost by Dying?: Collected Prose Poems, copyright 1992 by Robert Bly.

"Hearing Gary Snyder Read" was originally printed as a broadside by Alan Brilliant.

"A Day on the Sea," "The Thumb," "A Willow Leaf," "The Skull-Bone," "A Pine Tree," and "The Skin on a Horse's Neck" appear here for the first time.

The Marie Alexander Poetry Series

SERIES EDITOR: ROBERT ALEXANDER

Volume 12
Reaching Out to the World
Robert Bly

Volme 11
The House of Your Dream:
An International Collection of Prose Poetry
Edited by Robert Alexander and Dennis Maloney

Volume 10
Magdalena
Maureen Gibbon

Volume 9
The Angel of Duluth
Madelon Sprengnether

Volume 8
Light from an Eclipse
Nancy Lagomarsino

Volume 7
A Handbook for Writers
Vern Rutsala

Volume 6
The Blue Dress
Alison Townsend